Published by Creative Education
P.O. Box 227, Mankato, Minnesota 56002
Creative Education is an imprint of The Creative Company
www.thecreativecompany.us

Design and Production by The Design Lab
Printed in the United States of America

Photographs by Alamy (Covalart Photographic, Fotoart by Andy Marshall,
Xavier Henri (Fovea), SCPhotos), Getty Images (General Photographic
Agency, Stephane de Sakutin/AFP, Three Lions, Luis Veiga), The Granger
Collection, NY, iStockphoto (Jose Luis Gutierrez, Fanelie Rosier)

Library of Congress Cataloging-in-Publication Data
Riggs, Kate.
Eiffel tower / by Kate Riggs.
p. cm. — (Now that's big!)
Includes index.
ISBN 978-1-58341-702-7
1. Tour Eiffel (Paris, France)—Juvenile literature. 2. Paris (France)—
Buildings, structures, etc.—Juvenile literature. I. Title.
NA2930.R54 2009   725'.970944361—dc22   2007052338

First edition

9 8 7 6 5 4 3 2 1

TOWER

BY KATE RIGGS

The Eiffel (*EYE-full*) Tower is a tall tower. It is in Paris, France. The tower looks like a giant arrow pointing to the sky. It was named after the man who **designed** it, Gustave (*GOO-stahv*) Eiffel.

Eiffel had a simple but detailed design for the tower

6

Eiffel began designing the tower in 1887. He wanted to make it out of something strong. He did not want it to fall over! He chose metals like steel and iron.

1887

The tower's metal beams were all made in Eiffel's factory

8

It took 18,000 iron and steel beams to make the Eiffel Tower!

About 200 men built the Eiffel Tower. It was **dangerous** work. The workers had to lift the steel **beams** high in the air. Then they had to stack them in just the right places. It was like putting a huge puzzle together.

The Eiffel Tower was the tallest structure in the world when it was finished in 1889.

It took about a year and a half to build the Eiffel Tower. It had three levels that people could stand on. People could climb the stairs inside the tower until they were almost 1,000 feet (305 m) in the air!

The openings in the metal are called latticework (*LAT-us-werk*)

12

Gustave Eiffel wanted to make his simple tower beautiful. He put lots of pretty details on the metal.

The iron beams in the Eiffel Tower are full of holes. They are not solid. This lets the wind blow through the tower. Even if it is really windy, the tower will not fall down.

There is an elevator in each of the Eiffel Tower's four legs. Each elevator can hold 40 people.

People can see the beams up-close while riding the elevators

When people think of Paris, they think of the Eiffel Tower. Everyone who goes to Paris wants to see the Eiffel Tower. People wait in long lines to climb the stairs to one of the levels. Or they ride in elevators to the top.

The tower is in a park called the Champ (*SHAHM*) de Mars

Millions of people visit the Eiffel Tower every year. The tower had a lot of visitors in 1999. More than six million people toured the Eiffel Tower that year.

1999

Tour boats take people on the river past the Eiffel Tower

18

The Eiffel Tower stands close to a big river that goes through the middle of Paris.

Lots of people go to Paris in the summer. It is hot then. But the tower is open every day of the year.

The tall tower can be seen from almost anywhere in Paris

The Eiffel Tower soars above the city of Paris. It is hard to miss! There is no other building in the world quite like the Eiffel Tower.

French people celebrate their independence day (July 14) with fireworks at the Eiffel Tower.

GLOSSARY

beams—*long, strong pieces of metal that hold something up and keep it from falling*

dangerous—*something that is not safe*

designed—*drew up plans for*

independence—*freedom*

metals—*hard, shiny materials that can be made into different shapes to make things like buildings*

READ MORE ABOUT IT

Bardhan-Quallen, Sudipta. *The Eiffel Tower.* Farmington Hills, Mich.: KidHaven Press/ Thomson Gale, 2005.

Hayden, Kate. *Amazing Buildings.* New York: Dorling Kindersley, 2003.

24